GREEN EARTH

A POETIC TREE

SEMISI PONE

BSc, MSc (Hons). Auckland.

Note.

If you cannot find the meaning of words or ideas used in the poetry, try looking it up online!

Introduction.

The earth is very fragile. Many environmental, industrial and other problems, that affect nature, highlighted in the news, have to be overcome. These include the ozone hole which has probably closed according to some scientists. The greenhouse gases and sea level rise is another. I have seen a TV programme where they showed the sea bubbling out of the ground in Tuvalu. A small group of islands in the Pacific. It happens when the tide come in. Their crops fail from too much salt in the underground water. In neighboring Kiribati some island people, on the coastal villages, walk around in one foot deep water during high tide. The water has invaded their seaside village.

Deforestation is another problem. The carbon sinks of the world are slowly disappearing. Many organizations and activists work with logging companies to replant trees and avoid erosion and following problems.

Pollution from industry is an ongoing concern. Trading in Carbon Credits may solve it.

Only future generations will find out what the effects on the earth will be.

Chemicals and gases pollute rivers, the sea and the air continuously. It has caused acid rain in some places.

Pollution from farming is another. New Zealand has put in place some legislation to make farmers responsible for cleaner farm runoff. Hopefully they do the same in other farming countries.

With the global treaties to clean the environment our children and grandchildren will be able to enjoy the world of tomorrow.

Enjoy.

PART 1.

POEMS ABOUT ENVIRONMENTAL PROBLEMS OF THE WORLD.

GLOBAL WARMING

Lightning breathed life into inanimate
compounds, cells with no wife doing the rounds
Amoebas swim in the primordial soup
And evolve into animals dancing in a loop

They grew eyes and fins, mouths and swim
In search of food, it was plentifully good
Then they grew legs and climbed into the land
Gave rise to a monkey, the ancestor of man

The air was so clean their noses had no sieve
Diseases were rare no pollution there
The monkeys became smart and developed tools
Pollution were just farts and odor in their stool

They became more industrious and handsome
Converting raw materials to pass inviting foreign
workers to come, they build cities, vehicles and
trains drilled for oil and titties, and fly in
airplanes

Trees grew like weeds from the plentiful carbon
And shed all their leaves from acid rain and
warmth, the warm seas are killing the food chain
Scientists research the pieces concluding its
thawing ice, not rain

Sea level rise, islands go under, don't act
surprised if it drowns Kiribati
Fogs are common in all large towns
Environmentalists say its smog from all the
burning fires

Cancers are common from all the pollution
Be wise like King Solomon and create a solution
Many civilizations have gone before
And drowned in their pollution
Chemicals, CO_2, not just waste

Many organizations try to reverse the trend
SPREP and the United Nations and in many
other lands, here is still time to clean up the earth
Or we'll stand in line to farewell the dead
And return to the primordial soup from whence
we came, amoebas dancing in a loop with no one
to blame.

THE OXYGEN CYCLE

God said, let there be life
And it was done, Adam needs a wife
He was the only one, God took his rib bone
And created her
But she was mostly stoned, from the marijuana
air, she ate the forbidden fruit
And drove Adam to despair

They were banished from Eden
To wander the barren Earth
They learned to reproduce
And Eve gave birth
To Gain and Abel
Boys not angels

Their descendants
And all their animals
Breathed life to plants
The oxygen cycle
To keep them alive
Air from the primordial soup
Plants turning carbon into food.

THE FOOD CHAIN

Whales are so large
They break all scales
Eats plankton and fast
To reproduce in Wales

Fish eats plankton too
And provide food
For animals bigger than them
Energy channels, not a problem

The sun gives energy to plants
And the plankton
Waste chemicals from land
Also accumulating poisons

Man sits at the top
Accumulating poisons is his lot
From all the plants and animals
In the food chain.

ACID RAIN

It's like bald patches
In pictures from space
Dead trees like rashes
On a baby's face

Factories and vehicle smoke
React with clouds up above
To lower the pH
Creating acid rain on crops

It kills trees
Not just defoliating leaves
Destroys fishing fleets
From the empty seas

Dead rivers flow
Like the poisonous blood
Old men look like crows
Carcasses from Noah's flood.

OUR ISLANDS

Tuvalu is under water
Bubbling from the ground
Like lambs to the slaughter
The environment is the problem

The rising sea they showed on TV
Just one foot of water covering the floor
Of their houses and village
A terrible legacy of CO_2 emissions

The land is sinking, the people are afraid
This was their home for generations
Where should they go
If they cannot live here

Neighboring Kiribati is also suffering
Fiji has offered an island refuge
For those who want to emigrate
A friend in need is a friend indeed.

GREENHOUSE GASES.

Earth is a yolk
Surrounded by the white atmosphere
Keeping all waste gases in bulk
Trapping the sun's rays like solar flares

Forests are carbon sinks
Swallowing accumulating gases
Like having a drink
Assets for investors to purchase

Plant trees in the desert
To open your carbon account
Create paradise in places
With no trees to count

The rising temperature
May become normal
Reductions in expenditure
And regrowth of coral.

ENERGY

The Big Bang created
An expanding universe
Collapsing energy in places
Forming stars and planets

Nuclear fusion created the sun
Life giving energy to plants
Creating protein and carbohydrates
To feed the whole planet

Energy is passed on
To feeders and predators
Building bone, muscles, and neurons
Growing bigger than before

Some energy escape as heat
To warm their bodies
Their life cycle is complete
Nutrients for worms to eat

Plant roots absorb nutrients again
To create more food
And fulfill all of God's plans
Nature is so good

Only 5 billion years left
Of life giving energy from the sun
Then it will expand before death
And consume everyone

Earth will be no more
Energy return to space
We cannot destroy it
Nor create.

THE POLLUTED RIVER

Rivers run clear
With overhanging plants
Filled with fish and deer
Protein for everyone

Then they build a factory
To process the sheep and cattle
Powered by coal from ancient trees
Filling the air with soot like a kettle

Animals fart methane into the air
Their ammonia filled urine runoff
The river turns muddy and share
Stinking waste and fishes cough

New species arose
Others disappear
Artificial selection like prose
Evolution filled with tears.

DRIFTWOOD

The island people collect from their shores
Wood keep fires burning 'umu like before
A present from Maui and the Gods
Feeding people and their children

After 200 years there's no more wood just plastic
Bottles and plastic bags, floating nets under the
pier, no more gods, fire or magic
Birds drop from the sky, fish float in the seas
They ask the Doctors why they are filled with
poisons and cannot see

Now the seas bubbling up the cracks
Of the sandy ground, islands sink
Cannot export fish to overseas markets
None can be found

Crops fail each year, now they eat rice
Imported from Indonesia at a cheaper price
They have to leave their island
And live in another country
The environment's poisoned
Now they work, nothing is free

And the old people remembered
The stories of old, Maui and their gods
Which made their people bold
It is all they have left
Stories of their island history
Driftwood to fill their plates
Eating under a tree.

MANGROVES

Their roots breathe and hold silt there
Or the land will waste away
From the seas, waves and spray
Fish feed under their leaves
And sleep under trunks
Spawn between the roots
Providing predators with food

Coastal people use the wood
To build homes, pens and fires
Trap craps, sell more goods
To traders and labor for hire
Plant mangroves around the island
Its roots are strong to bind your land together
Once grown, hurricanes will not matter

Its oil once grace royal approval
Stories of ancient cultures in the Pacific
Where it grows and protect many islands
Provide for coastal people and their village
Its seed travel the waves and settle in far places
Island beaches, river banks or new reefs
To build up and nourish new land.

THE OZONE HOLE.

Scientists say we need the ozone layer
To keep out ultraviolet rays
Which may cause cancer
But it's being depleted
By CFCs and other gases
From spray cans and fridges

O_3 is the formula
Just 3 oxygen molecules
Bound together to provide
A protective shield for earth
And give hope to the future of man
We will last a bit longer

The ozone hole has closed again
Man's effort is rewarded
Our understanding of the cosmos
Is the key to saving our planet
And control of the firmament
In a million years we'll still be here.

THE POLES

The North and South Poles are so cold
Rain will freeze in the air
Just like tear drops on a statue
Much of Earth's water are collected there

The Arctic and Antarctic ice area
Are bigger than Australia
If all that ice melt
It will drown many islands in the world

A few degrees rise in temperature
Is all it needs
Increase all expenditure
Confine hot air to the beach

A dog pants to cool itself
The atmosphere lets out heat
To cool the world
But a blanket of CO_2 will be a disaster.

Our environment is very frail
Unseen dangers with no trails
It's good we understand
Keep nature in balance is the plan.

THE DEAD REEF

They say it was a hurricane
That killed the reef
But there was none in our area
Perhaps its agricultural urea

Scientists tested the water
No poisons were found
Just increases in temperature
Silent killers with no sound

The sun, giver of energy and life
Provide nice tans for your wife
Is the source of the heat
The ozone hole we cannot beat

Everything is safe
When nature is balanced
Man is in strife
From his own activities.

DEFORESTATION

The Amazon forest
Helps clean the air
By absorbing CO_2
Greenhouse gases too

CO_2 is turned into oxygen
Carbohydrates and water
Cooling the air like a fan
Air conditioned fodder

Then commercial logging
Clears vast areas of forest
With slow replanting
Carbon account arrears

 In Papua New Guinea and Asia
Africa, Solomon Islands and Indonesia
Logging moves at a fast rate
With new trees to replace.

PART 2.

POEMS ABOUT POVERTY.

POVERTY

When I was young we lived in town
All the food was made of flour
Or rice and sugar three times a day
No nutrition experts to advise

In the villages, they had fruit
Yams, pigs, chicken and seafood
There was money from the tourists
Crops, melons and fishing

My Dad worked for the government
We were considered rich
A large house, louvers and a fridge
Cooking with electricity, kerosene or twigs

He made $60 per week
A high salary in town
But buying power was weak
Cook the pancakes till brown

Every Sunday we had 'umu
Root crops, raw fish and meat in leaves
Pawpaw for dessert
Immersed in coconut cream

During Christmas I had toys
And roasted pig by the boys
Camp in Church during the weekend
And eat till you burst

Then I went overseas
They say we are poor
We sleep under trees
And fish with no lure

Kids go to school with no lunch
Refuse to obey the rules
Truants with dope smoke
No food stunts their minds

Billions of dollars
Are spent on the roads
Laborers not scholars
Whiskey to warm their throats.

Training fools is their choice
Deeds with no voice
Stunted brains cannot work
Smoking marijuana for a break

A Police State in the making
Dictators in secret
Everyone needs money
It's the world economy

Poverty exists in the mind
Read Oliver Twist, Dickens is more fun
I just cannot remember
Which part was mine

It's what people do
That makes a difference
Lock your kids in the loo
Or become friends

Empowering people is the aim
Use skills to solve problems
When you have nothing
Be more creative

Convert the sand into oil
Plant taro instead of corn
Protein and vitamin from the leaves
Carbohydrate from the corm

Don't eat steaks everyday
Try fried rice with eggs
It's a quarter of the cost
The same value for less

Plant your own vegetables
To save money for food
Drink 6 beers instead of 20
Cook wholesome meals

Your wealth is in your brain
It controls your body
And keep you sane
Train it to be ready

Nothing is worth more
Than yourself
Treat it with respect
Always save time to reflect.

WE ARE ALL MILLIONAIRES

I have 104,000 hours to sell
It's worth one million dollars
If one hour is worth $10
Sell half to invest
And live on the rest
The minimum wage is $20

In Australia, one hour is worth more
Invest two million
And be richer than before
Donate a dollar to the United Nations
Make 350 billion for foreign relations
Help the world to be better

There will be no poverty
All nations will be rich
We all pay for our uses
All sweet, no abuse
Go for a holiday
Smile all the way

In Africa there's no rain
Water the crops from the tap
Tow a few icebergs there
And fill the tanks to the brim
No problems, sing some hymns
God is kind to Christians

There are no problems
In the world of history
Only Pol Pots and their girls
They leave skeletons in every cupboard
The wishes of their Lords
Who command attention

They do not wish
To make you rich
Only slaves in their schemes
It gives their small brains power
To see you in pain and suffer
Says the Conspiracy Theory

More money are in the hands
Of a few rich people
Than all the population of Africa
They do not want solutions
To empower the masses
Only disease, death and pollution.

THE VILLAGE FISHERMAN

He wakes early in the morning
To check his fish traps
And sell some strings for money
School fees, bus fares and bags

His four children are in High School
They dream of a better future
A government job in town
Or become a doctor

But Mum says, go overseas
And visit your uncle
Get a job with him
At the shopping mall

They all become cleaners
At Westfield, Auckland
Still high achievers
With idle land.

THE COMIC POLICEMAN

They call him Mr Bean
A guitarist for Queen
He did not play
Just singing was all he can

He likes to show his power
And sing in the shower
But never play the guitar
Feeling like a czar

Patrolling the neighborhood
And come across some loot
Hid it in a deposit box
And blamed the local fox

The local widow is his honey
Always give her money
And kisses for the children
Collecting charity for Jesus.

CHURCH CHARITY

I spend nine years
Collecting bread for charity
Every Sunday before some beers
It seems like eternity

Budget organizations estimate
Increases in financial difficulties
Collect bread from your mate
Save money for the family

Queues at the Salvation Army
Are getting longer
Food parcels disappear quickly
They need food more

Lessons in poverty
Exercises in liberty
It's your own choice
If you have hungry boys.

THE PLANTER.

He plants yam, taro and cassava
Vegetables and maybe some kumara
Some pigs are in the pen
Chickens and a few hens

The family has a van
With plenty of root crops and melons
Selling the extra crops to make money
In the village he is doing well

The Rugby Committee
Selected him to the National Team
They toured Australia and Fiji
New Zealand and Britain

He scored one try
But their team got fried
By all the other teams
They lost by 150 points but tried.

THE BUSKER

Singing is her profession
And playing musical instruments
Fans stand at attention
She has many friends

Traveling the country
And the cities of the world
Singing to all who will listen
Playing the guitar so well

At the end of each day
She counts her earnings
One thousand dollars for today
Or just a few shillings

It is a good earner
She writes and paints as a learner
What's all that complaint
About unemployment?.

THE FARMER

His grandfather was a share milker
Who bought a 2,000 hectare farm
Selling milk to Fonterra
And make $400,000

Everything is going well
He also won his dream girl
Then the price of milk fell
And he has to sell

Moving into town
Was the jewel in the crown
But all the diamonds fell off
They were worse off than Maddoff

It was another Crafar farm
With no hope of a rebound
Asking for a benefit was the last
Kick in the guts.

THESE WERE THE DAYS.

Tommy was a laborer
Earning $11 per hour
It was the highest pay
He could command in those days

Working for families
Gave him $500 for his children
Every week for shopping
There were 10 of them

It was the best policy
Of the Labour Government
Assistance for the needy
Intervention where it counts

Then he won the lotto
A trick by the Police
365 reasons to leave town
And come back for another round.

STREET PROFESSIONAL

He was a professional
Earning $100,000 a year
He lost his job
And could not afford a beer

After years of looking
Moved to the street
Living under bridges
Shattered dream of riches

They looked for him for years
No address, no phone, no email
Finally meeting in tears
Moss grew on his nails

Years of inactivity
Drove him crazy
He thinks like a pro
But talks like a whore.

PART 3.

POEMS ABOUT SUCCESS AND DREAMS.

NAPOLEON I

A soldier from Corsica
With 7 siblings
He became the Emperor
They became Kings

Constantly at war
With his neighbors
Remarried Marie of Austria
Won battles with Prussia

Initiator of Laws
And Public structures
Lost at Waterloo
Exiled to Elba

Back for 100 days
And lost again
This time exiled to St Helens
Where he passed away.

SWEET SUCCESS

He grew up in the Pacific
OECD rate his country as poor
But everybody was happy
They work hard and got more

He passed all his exams
Everything went according to plan
Traveled to Auckland University
And got 2 degrees

Worked for MAFF
And the USP
SPC and IPPC
Then retired at 33.

THE COMMONWEALTH

They share all their money
And worldly belongings
53 countries, formerly colonies
The British build up their wealth

Annual Finance Ministers meetings
Biannual Heads meet
To decide all activities
In Education, Agriculture, Science

Countries come in
Others go out
Depends on misbehaving
And breaking the rules

Encouraging scholarship
In the young people
Scientists to create sheep
Producing more meat

Commonwealth students
Learn the history of Britain
Aspire to attend Oxford and Cambridge
Work harder and become rich

They leave their traditions behind
And adopt the Westminster Style
Constitutions and the rule of law
No more executions like before

Their countries grew in wealth
Better Health, Education and Trade
Only dreams to create
With nothing to regret.

BROKEN DREAMS

I dream of being rich
And end up a pauper
I dream of being King
But only changed a diaper

Many people are lost
In the land of broken dreams
Singing songs of Babylon
Under trees by the stream

They long for a cruise
On the QEII
See the islands of paradise
Antarctica too

Keep sailing to the East
Throw the fishing line
Catch a shark's dream
And eat them alive

Then become a star
In somebody else's dream
You will go far
Singing Babylon by the stream.

SEE SEE

I see you today
Come out and play
I see you tomorrow
With money to borrow
I see you next day
Doctor wants a replay
"I'm not crazy anymore
Being stupid is such a bore"

I see you next week
With a slap on your cheek
I see you next month
With some food for your mouth
I see you next year
With some salt like King Lear
I see you next century
"Sorry, don't come I won't be here".

PART 4.

MISCELLANEOUS POEMS.

PIG TRAP

A bald man
With a grudge
Is no fun to be around
She might drop you with a punch

Kaka is his name
Playing robber is his game
Greedy as Ebeneza
Alladin's lamp is his treasure

A policeman is just a laborer
He has not learned to think
Cannot be a Prime Minister
Or become a treasurer

Taking orders is his lot
To investigate or confiscate pot
The Manager is the thinker
Working out not a drinker

Many wrongs cannot be right
Watch your back it's a knife
Be transparent and honest
Or fight for your life

His instrument
Is the stupid wife
They force her hand
With no right to understand.

FIGHTING GAME

Fight for life
Or lose your wife
Cancer is a knockout punch
There's no time for another round

Raise more money for research
Tumors take no prisoners
Always look under the breast
We'll knock it out with a sonar

Diseases are his weapons
Infecting people like a moron
And kick them out of work
Suffering tickles his mirth.

INTELLIGENT AMOEBA.

The spermatozoa swam in the dark
Through the womb towards the egg
Fusing to form a fetus
Another human Prometheus

It grabbed the wall of the womb
And stuck to it like in a tomb
For nine months it grew and rolled
Getting ready in a ball

Then it heard its mother's cry
To move out it must be a sign
Dropping out to suck air
Exhausting as if in despair

First he learned to suck milk
Then cry for everything he needs
He became a little boy
Fascinated with his toys

As a young man
He enjoys the women
Talk, walk, dinner then fight
What's the point of being right?

His children call him Dad
The wife drives him mad
White hairs are on his crown
He left one day and cannot be found

Now he walks with a stick
Teasing his neighbor to show his wit
He does not cry anymore
Although walking make him sore

Then one day he woke up
Beside St Peter with a pup
Welcome to heaven, he said
You'll be happy we're not bad.

THE SHOW

Jump from space
Break the speed of sound
Take Lennox Lewis
Through another round

Bomb the twin towers
And start a war
Eat $1 trillion dollars
Like a hungry boar

Go to Hollywood
And create a movie
Lord of the Rings, Avatar
Jaws, Dinosaurs, The Conqueror

Run for President
Of your country
Import some voters
Sex for free

Become King of the World
In the new Order
United Nations with no borders
Or migrate to Jupiter

Convert the sea
Into oil
Save the world
And the collect the spoils.

NOTES ABOUT THE AUTHOR.

Semisi Pule also known as Semisi Pule Pone graduated from the University of Auckland with a Bachelor of Science in 1985 and a Master of Science in 1989. He worked for the Ministry of Agriculture, Fisheries and Forests, Tonga, as a research Plant Pathologist and Senior Plant Virologist from June, 1985 to February 1992. He was a Fellow at the University of the South Pacific, Samoa Agriculture Campus, Institute for Research, Extension and Training in Agriculture from March 1992 to May 1993. In June 1993 he was appointed the Plant Protection Officer/Advisor and Co-ordinator for the South Pacific Commission's Plant Protection Service in Suva, Fiji. During his time there he also did some work for the United Nations Food and Agriculture Organization in Global Plant Quarantine Standards and Regional Plant Protection Organizations. He moved to New Zealand in 1996 and started a business. He also did a lot of other work in the last 20 years. Some of his experience is written in books like **"If you can't find a job start a business"** with the aim of helping unemployed people and poems, sprinkled with some humor. His other poems also reflect some of his experience with various organizations. He also writes children's stories with the series **"The Children of the Gods"** the first one. It is a series of 10 books telling the story with 3 completed so far. He also writes humor, religion, science and self improvement books.

He publishes and distributes his books under Rainbow Enterprises Books.

www.ingramcontent.com/pod-product-compliance
Lightning Source LLC
LaVergne TN
LVHW051712080426
835511LV00017B/2871